Welcome to Te Papa

Haere mai ki Te Papa

Te Papa's roofline
unfolds towards
the sea.

Haere mai,
e te manuhiri tūārangi,
haere mai ki tēnei marae …

———

Welcome, visitors,
to this marae,
this meeting place …

You will hear these words at the beginning of a pōwhiri, a welcoming ceremony. They are part of a karanga, a call that invites you onto the host community's ground. So begins an encounter between a home people and their visitors. A pōwhiri establishes or renews connections and prepares the way for hosts and guests to come together.

Welcome to Te Papa. We will look after you on our home ground. Our many official hosts are here to guide you or answer your questions, wherever in the Museum you may be.

Te Papa is the guardian of Aotearoa New Zealand's national collections — from great art works to specimens of the tiniest plants and animals. We invite you to share them with us.

OUR PLACE – TE PAPA

The Museum of New Zealand Te Papa Tongarewa is
New Zealand's national museum, known as Te Papa,
or Our Place.

The word 'papa' has various meanings, including 'container' and
'site'. Te Papa Tongarewa can be translated as 'the place where treasured
things are held'. You could think of it as a massive six-storey treasure box.

Te Papa opened in 1998, a new museum with a new vision that brought
together the collections of the former National Museum and the
National Art Gallery (founded in 1936). Te Papa now welcomes more
than 1.5 million visitors every year.

Te Papa's philosophy, or kaupapa, emphasises the living face behind its cultural treasures, many of which retain deep ancestral links to Māori, New Zealand's tangata whenua, the people of the land. The Museum recognises the partnership that was created by the signing of the Treaty of Waitangi, te Tiriti o Waitangi, in 1840.

From the Museum's earliest planning, Te Papa has worked in partnership with Māori; that's why the marae is the focal point of both the building and the organisation. The Museum works hard to be bicultural and to recognise the Treaty in all that it does.

TE PAPA AND THE CAPITAL

Last, loneliest, loveliest … Aotearoa New Zealand is far away from so much of the world.

Together the two main islands and various smaller islands of Aotearoa New Zealand are more than 1600 kilometres in length, about 450 kilometres at the widest, and cover more than 15,000 kilometres of coastline. Its regional interests extend to the Kermadec and sub-Antarctic islands and to Antarctica itself. New Zealand is similar in size to Japan or the United Kingdom, yet has a population of fewer than 4.5 million.

Te Papa is located in New Zealand's capital city, Wellington, where it stands like a sturdy island on the edge of the city's great harbour, Te Whanganui-a-Tara. Wellington is a pocket-sized capital, tucked around a harbour, winding up through narrow valleys and spilling across steep hills.

Is Wellington truly the windiest capital city in the world? Well, it would hardly be surprising, given its location on the roaring forties westerly wind belt, the funnelling influence of Cook Strait and the hilly terrain. What's more, Wellington sits on one of New Zealand's major fault lines; earthquakes are common. It can be wild, windy *and* shaky here!

► The New Zealand Post Museum Collection, gifted to Te Papa in 1992, contains many rare stamps, stamp sheets, proofs and original artwork dating from 1855, when New Zealand first issued stamps. This 'Tiki Tour of New Zealand No. 2' 70 cent stamp sheet was released in 2012.

THE BUILDING

Te Papa rises from Wellington's waterfront like a rugged island. The north face overlooks the harbour, and from its bluff-like walls there's an embracing view of sea, hills and sky. Just like an island, it takes everything that's thrown at it: intense sunlight, frequent gales, driving rain and salt-laden air.

A massive grey wall faces west, dividing the building and emerging towards the south like a buttress, echoing the fault line that runs parallel to it through the city and along the western side of the harbour.

The wall's shape also suggests a canoe hauled up on land, stern to the city and prow to the sea. This refers to the arrival of voyagers, both ancient and modern. The Museum is both a landing place and a launch pad for ideas and experience.

The Museum was designed by a New Zealand architecture practice, Jasmax, which won a competition for its design in 1990. It was built on unstable waterfront land: consolidating the site took eight months of continual pounding by a 25-tonne weight.

New Zealand materials have been used wherever possible. The oatmeal-coloured cladding is dolomite from Nelson, the black basalt of the diagonal wall is from Auckland, and the interior timbers are the native woods mataī, rewarewa, tawa and kauri, as well as macrocarpa and New Zealand-grown eucalyptus.

TE MARAE

Te Papa's marae, Rongomaraeroa, is a fully functioning communal centre, run according to Māori kawa or protocol. It is the heart of Museum life — a place for welcomes, celebrations and ceremonies. It is also a living exhibition, showcasing contemporary Māori art and design.

The marae comprises an outside space, the marae ātea, or place of encounter, and the wharenui, the meeting house. The name of the wharenui is Te Hono ki Hawaiki, which speaks of the connection with Hawaiki (the place of spiritual origin for Māori).

Te Hono ki Hawaiki was designed and constructed by 40 carvers from around New Zealand, led by Te Papa's first kaihautū, the artist Cliff Whiting. His contemporary approach to design, colour and materials is an evolution of customary wharenui design. The wharenui includes carved ancestral figures as well as carvings that depict the occupations and origins of Pākehā and other newcomers to New Zealand.

Rongomaraeroa is a magnificent setting for Te Papa's promotion of the festival of Matariki as an indigenous celebration in which all New Zealanders can share. Matariki, the Māori New Year, is enjoying a cultural revival; marking the reappearance of Matariki, the Pleiades star cluster, in southern hemisphere skies in June, it is a time of both contemplation and celebration.

Visitors of all cultures can feel at home in this contemporary marae.

▶ Te Hono ki Hawaiki, Te Papa's wharenui or meeting house.

Te Papa's unique marae, Rongomaraeroa, is a place where all cultures can come together.

The marae also represents Te Ao Mārama. In Māori tradition, this is the world of light, where living things dwell. Papatūānuku, the Earth mother, and Ranginui, the sky father, are the original parents who formed the world. They lived in the light, but they clung together, and their children lived in the darkness of their parents' embrace.

Some of the children became restless. They tried to separate their mother from their father, but they could not. Eventually, one of the sons, Tāne, placed his head against Papatūānuku and his feet against Ranginui and forced them apart. In so doing he opened the world of light and created a space for all living things.

The marae floor symbolises Papatūānuku, with Ranginui represented in Robert Jahnke's floor-to-ceiling glass doors. The raising of these doors evokes Tāne separating his parents.

Cliff Whiting's striking contemporary carvings in the wharenui Te Hono ki Hawaiki are topped by demi-god Māui and his brothers capturing the sun.

► The massive glass doors of Rongomaraeroa, designed by sculptor Robert Jahnke, represent Ranginui, the sky father.

FORUM FOR THE NATION

Te Papa has an important role as a 'forum for the nation', giving voice to the people who are connected with the Museum's treasures as a way of representing the dynamism and continual evolution of culture.

New Zealanders include not only the original people of the land and the second wave of arrivals (mostly Europeans), who have long-standing cultures in this country, but also more recent arrivals from Asia, Africa and South America. Most come by choice. Some, refugees from extremes of conflict, emerge here at the end of an escape chute.

The idea of tūrangawaewae, a place to stand, features strongly in Māori culture. It has greatly influenced Te Papa's aspiration to be a place where all New Zealanders feel a sense of belonging, a tūrangawaewae for all who continue to come and live in New Zealand.

► A view towards the meeting place of Earth, sea and sky through Rongomaraeroa's waharoa, a tribute to all New Zealand's voyagers.

Te Papa celebrated its 25-millionth visitor in 2015.

The oldest object in Te Papa's collection is the fossil of a jawless fish that lived about 470–480 million years ago.

THE COLLECTIONS – NGĀ KOHINGA TAONGA

At any one time, there are 25 to 30 different exhibitions on display at Te Papa. Some such as Rongomaraeroa, the marae, are part of the Museum's fabric, while *Bush City*, the 'living exhibition' outside, just keeps on growing!

Most of Te Papa's exhibits are drawn from its collections, but the displays are just a fraction of its holdings. Behind the scenes are millions of biological specimens, art works, cultural treasures, historical objects, documents and images, all carefully stored – a treasure trove of information for research and a legacy for future generations.

Te Papa specialises in a broad subject: Aotearoa New Zealand. As the national museum, it must answer a big question: 'What is unique, distinctive and typical about this country – its environment, its native animals and plants, its history, its people and their ways of life?'

The collections are organised into five areas: Natural Environment, Taonga Māori (Māori cultural treasures), New Zealand History, Pacific Cultures and Art.

▶ Te Papa's collection ranges from the massive to the minute. These specimens are from the Museum's foreign beetle collection.

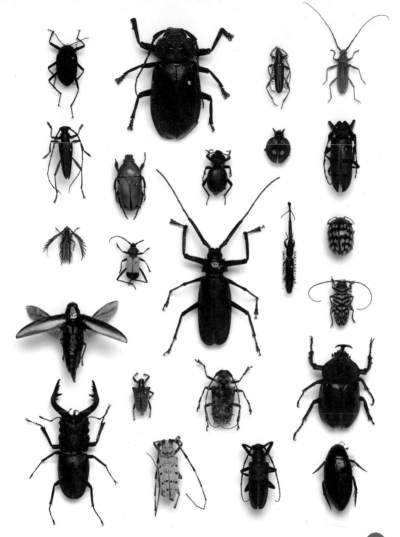

Te Papa Open Day at one of the Museum's Tory Street storerooms.

EARTHQUAKES

Zealandia, New Zealand's continental mass, includes all the islands above the waves and a far larger submerged expanse. In fact, only seven percent of 'Zealandia' is above the sea, and much of this was formed — and is still forming — as a result of the dynamic interaction between two tectonic plates.

The North Island sits on the Australian Plate. The Pacific Plate to the east is slowly forcing its way underneath the Australian Plate, producing a volcanic zone. Lake Taupō, for example, is the crater of a massive volcano, whose last major eruption, 1800 years ago, caused weather abnormalities recorded in Rome and China.

Along much of the South Island, the two plates grind past each other (rather than one under the other) at around 40 millimetres a year — as fast as fingernails grow. In Earth terms, that's a full sprint. As the plates collide, the land is pushed up, creating the Southern Alps.

Seismographs record about 14,000 earthquakes in and around New Zealand each year. About 150 of these tremors are near enough or strong enough for people to feel them. But don't worry about an earthquake hitting while you are inside Te Papa. The Museum's 64,000-tonne structure is connected to its foundations by 135 'base isolators'. Made of rubber and lead, they absorb much of the ground's shaking during an earthquake. In an extremely powerful earthquake the bearings would allow the building to vibrate as much as half a metre in any direction.

► In the 'Earthquake House' in the popular *Awesome Forces* exhibition, a simulated aftershock gives visitors a taste of living on these shaky isles.

HABITATS

New Zealand has an extraordinary diversity of habitats, from dramatic mountainous peaks and active volcanoes to alluvial plains, lush temperate rainforests and dry inland grasslands. There are also sandy beaches, rugged coastlines, fiords, farmland, lakes and rivers, glaciers, geothermal areas (complete with geysers, steam and boiling mud) and rolling hill country. Quite a mix!

Moisture from the surrounding ocean supplies New Zealand with generous rain, which flows into forests, lakes, wetlands and rivers. The mountainous spine that runs through much of the country directs the weather, creating wetter areas in the west and drier areas in the east.

With a diversity of landscapes comes a diversity of climates, and in consequence a great diversity of nature. Alpine plants and animals, for example, have to cope with mountain extremes, while kauri forests luxuriate in the warm, wet northern climate. Rainforests are thick with plants twining over each other as they scramble for their place in the light. In the dense crowns of canopy trees, gardens of climbing and perching species flourish high above the forest floor.

Te Papa's natural history collections document the unique inhabitants of these diverse environments. Museum scientists use the latest technology to track changes in their distribution, identify where rare and threatened species are found, and monitor the spread of pests and weeds.

Aotearoa New Zealand's natural ecosystems are rich with life. Measured in one New Zealand forest were: 333 kilograms of earthworms per hectare of soil, and 145 kilograms of insects, mites, litter hoppers, spiders, millipedes and centipedes per hectare of leaf litter. And Te Papa has lots of them!

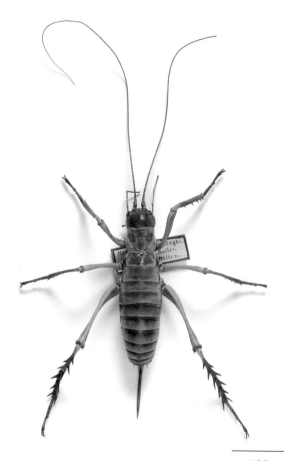

Wētā are unique to New Zealand. This West Coast bush wētā, collected in 1895, has an 85-millimetre-long body.

Taxonomy, or the identification and naming of new species, is a core part of Te Papa's scientific work. These early specimens of kōwhai (*Sophora tetraptera*, above) and silver fern (*Cyathea dealbata*, opposite) were collected by botanists Joseph Banks and Daniel Solander on James Cook's first voyage to New Zealand in 1769. Banks and Solander collected and named more than 360 specimens, many of which were previously unknown to European botanists.

Cyathea dealbata: Sw.

Polypodium excelsum. Mj.

31

Bush City, Te Papa's outside living exhibition, was planted with about 1400 trees, shrubs, ferns and other plants that are native to the Wellington area.

NATIVE SPECIES

New Zealand has been cut off from other land masses for at least 50 million years, and this long separation has resulted in the evolution of unique ecosystems. More than three-quarters of New Zealand's flowering plant species occur naturally only here, and before people arrived around 70 percent of bird species were found nowhere else.

Notable endemic species include the mighty kauri tree, which grows 50 metres tall and 6 metres in diameter; kākāpō, the world's only flightless parrot; tuatara, a reptile survivor from the dinosaur age; and large carnivorous snails.

Evidence suggests that the ancestors of some of these living things hitched a ride with Zealandia when it split from the supercontinent Gondwana. Others may have floated, flown or been blown here.

For millions of years, birds were the largest land-dwellers in New Zealand. They faced neither threat nor competition from mammals, and so a great number of species, such as the kiwi, gradually abandoned flight for life at ground level. Most extraordinary of the ground-dwellers were the moa, which ranged from the size of a large dog to giants that would have towered over humans.

The pay-off was more food for a less energetic lifestyle. But uniqueness can mean vulnerability in changed circumstances. Many of New Zealand's native species struggle to survive alongside people and their introduced plants and animals; moa, for example, were extinct by about 1400 AD.

► Specimens of giant native land snails (*Powelliphanta lignaria*), found in native bush in the South Island and southern North Island.

Many native New Zealand species could not withstand introduced predators and are now extinct or endangered. Here (clockwise from left) are the extinct laughing owl or whekau (*Sceloglaux albifacies*), the endangered lesser short-tailed bat or pekapeka (*Mystacina tuberculata*) and the endangered North Island kiwi (*Apteryx mantelli*).

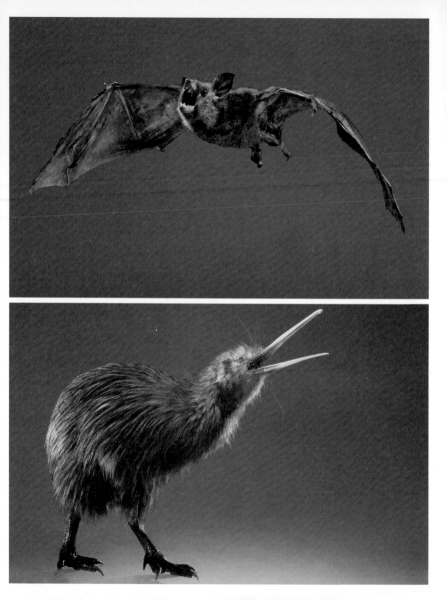

FAMOUS SKELETONS

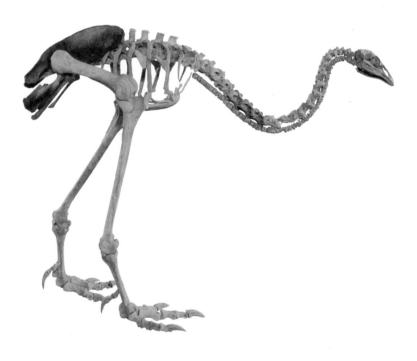

Moa, New Zealand's largest flightless birds, were hunted to extinction by early Māori settlers. This skeleton of an upland moa (*Megalapteryx didinus*) had been lying in a limestone cave in the South Island of New Zealand for 15,000 years when it was discovered in March 1987. Nine species of moa of varying sizes roamed New Zealand; this specimen stood about 1 metre tall.

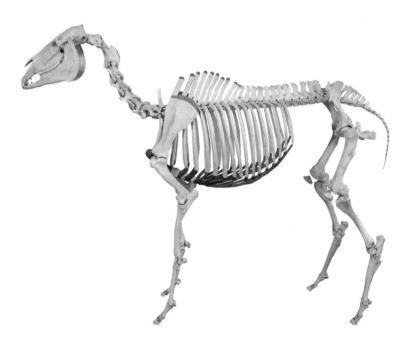

The skeleton of the legendary race horse Phar Lap is one of Te Papa's most popular exhibits. Born near Timaru in 1926 then moved to Australia, Phar Lap is renowned for his stellar racing career – he won 33 of his last 35 races. Phar Lap's mounted skin is on display at Melbourne Museum and his 6.3-kilogram heart is at the National Museum of Australia in Canberra.

THE SEA

New Zealand's seas are rich in life — algae, plankton, crustaceans, molluscs, fishes, birds and marine mammals.

New Zealand's oceans have supported a great number of marine species. Endemic whale and seal species are Hector's dolphin, the New Zealand sea lion and Māui's dolphin. The diversity of New Zealand's marine ecosystems is protected by its 34 marine reserves, which include the newest around the Kermadec Islands.

Large whales and other species, such as great white sharks and tunas, migrate through New Zealand's waters on their way between breeding grounds in the tropical Pacific and feeding grounds in the Antarctic. New Zealand is a stranding hotspot for whales.

The ocean also supports a profusion of seabirds; it's no wonder that New Zealand is sometimes called the seabird capital of the world. Great oceanic travellers such as albatrosses soar above the waters, shearwaters dip and dive, and penguins wing along swiftly underwater.

The fishing industry is of major importance to New Zealand. Te Papa scientists are part of the research that supports the industry's sustainability. They have documented more than 1200 fish species in New Zealand waters and improved the accurate identification of all commercial and bycatch species. The fishing industry has also helped Te Papa by collecting a wide range of scientific specimens, including the 4-metre-long, 470-kilogram colossal squid discovered in 2013.

► More than 1200 species of fish in New Zealand waters have been documented by Te Papa scientists. Shown here (from top to bottom) are the Southern seadevil (*Ceratias tentaculatus*), Perch (*Perca fluviatilis*), Brownspot bigeye (*Priacanthus macracanthus*) and Jock Stewart (*Helicolenus percoides*).

41

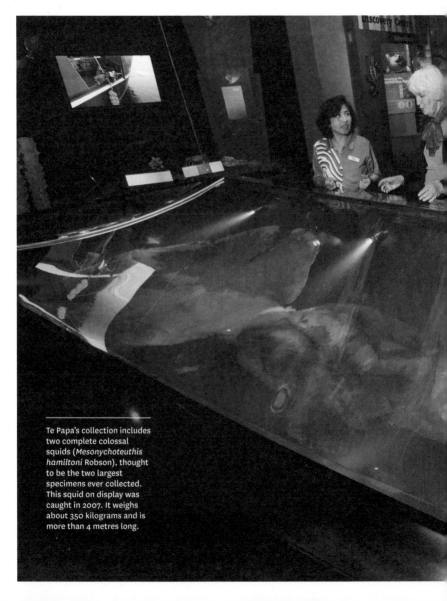

Te Papa's collection includes
two complete colossal
squids (*Mesonychoteuthis
hamiltoni* Robson), thought
to be the two largest
specimens ever collected.
This squid on display was
caught in 2007. It weighs
about 350 kilograms and is
more than 4 metres long.

ANCIENT TREASURES

Te Papa houses a number of ancient treasures. Dinosaurs feature in the form of an *Iguanodon* tooth (above), from 132–137 million years ago, and a mosasaur skull (opposite, above), from about 75 million years ago, discovered in 1980 in Hawke's Bay. The giant ammonite (*Lytoceras taharoaense*) (opposite, below), is the world's largest ammonite from the Jurassic period and is believed to be 160–165 million years old. Te Papa's Egyptian Mehit-em-Wesekht coffin dates from about 300 BCE.

Natural Environment

The Museum from the harbour edge, with Mount Victoria rising behind.

EARLY VOYAGERS

Forsaken homelands, long journeys and new opportunities are part of every New Zealander's history. Everyone who comes here must cross vast seas. Even today, with instant internet links and jet travel, migrating to such a far-off place requires huge commitment.

Around 800 years ago, New Zealand's islands became the last significant land masses to be settled by people. The origin of the first settlers is known as Hawaiki – a geographical location as well as a spiritual domain. These voyagers, the ancestors of Māori, travelled 4000 kilometres from eastern Polynesia, a journey that took several weeks.

Their waka hourua, ocean-going craft, were double-hulled, with a central deck. These expert navigators were guided by the waves, swells and currents, by signs of life in the air and water, by cloud types, and by the sun, moon and stars.

In recent years, the feats of the early voyagers have been recreated by their descendants. Hekenukumai Busby and his crews have built and sailed replica waka hourua between New Zealand, Tahiti, Rarotonga and Hawai'i, in both directions.

According to accounts of Kupe, the earliest named voyager to these parts, his wife, Kuramārōtini, spotted the distinctive clouds that form above land. 'He ao, he ao tea, he ao tea roa!' she called. 'Clouds, white clouds, long white clouds!' This is the origin of one of the names for this country: Aotearoa, 'land of the long white cloud'.

► According to Māori tradition, this large punga, named Te Maungaroa, is one of two anchor stones brought from Hawaiki by the Polynesian navigator Kupe.

The Moriori people are believed to have migrated directly from eastern Polynesia, and settled on Rēkohu (Chatham Island) and the nearby Rangihaute (Pitt Island), off the east coast of New Zealand. There they invented these waka pūhara, or wash-through canoes, for short voyages in the rough seas between their islands, and to hunt albatross, seals and fish. The sea would wash right through the vessel without swamping it. This 19th-century, 3-metre model of a waka pūhara is made from flax flower stalks, bracken fern and wood.

POLYNESIAN SETTLERS

The early Polynesian settlers in New Zealand came from tropical islands, but the new islands of Aotearoa were vast, cold and mountainous. The seasons were more sharply defined and the weather extremely variable.

The immediate challenges were huge. How to adapt their housing and clothing for cold conditions? How to replace tools and equipment? And what to do when imported crops failed to thrive?

The challenges came with rewards. Land and sea offered plentiful food. Native fern root, for example, was a widely available source of starch, and large birds such as the moa provided a source of protein.

Suddenly, native plant and animal communities that had evolved slowly over millions of years were sharing space and food resources with a predatory species. Humans brought a host of new plant and animal species, such as the Pacific rat and dog, and had mastered the use of fire.

The newcomers were also farmers. They cleared the land, opening it up for their crops such as kūmara (sweet potato).

Over generations, however, these early settlers learned to balance their survival needs with the environment's ability to provide for them.

► This waharoa, or gateway, is one of the first objects to greet visitors to Te Papa. Carved in about 1906 by master carver Neke Kapua (1871–c.1920, Ngāti Tarāwhai) and his sons, it was inspired by a waharoa that stood in the great pā Maketu in the Bay of Plenty.

MĀORI CARVING – NGĀ MAHI A RUA

Early settlers from Polynesia brought carving techniques and patterns with them. However, over generations, a distinctive style of Māori carving evolved, in part no doubt because of New Zealand's isolation.

In terms of wood, the first people were spoilt for choice. But finding materials for durable cutting edges was a challenge. Shell and bone were plentiful, but there was no ready substitute for the high-quality pearl shell widely used in the tropics. Obsidian and a hard form of argillite, quarried from a few sites and then traded, were soon in widespread use.

The most prized stone for carving was pounamu, a variety of jade also known as greenstone, which is found in the waterways of the western South Island. Te Wai Pounamu (Waters of Greenstone) is one of the South Island's names.

Over the centuries, and before the advent of metal technology, Māori took the art of shaping stone, wood and bone to extraordinary heights, and distinctive regional styles evolved. Metal tools, with their sharper and more easily sharpened edges, transformed carving practice and styles. Cuts could be made deeper and more defined, and substantial projects, such as large buildings, became practicable.

Adornments, tools, containers, weapons, architectural features, sacred objects – all are invested with the spirit of their makers and owners. They are among Te Papa's greatest treasures. Today, the customary carving arts thrive, handed down by masters at highly regarded schools.

► This Tā Moko panel was created by master carver Tene Waitere (c.1853–1931, Ngāti Tarāwhai) in about 1896. Commissioned by August Hamilton to illustrate tattoo patterns, or moko, in his book on Māori art, its use of naturalism and sculptural forms makes it Waitere's most innovative work.

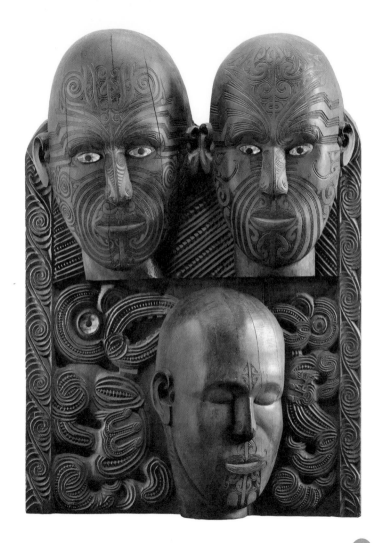

Tuhiwai is the famous mere pounamu, or greenstone weapon, of Te Rauparaha, the celebrated warrior chief of Ngāti Toa. Deadly weapons, mere were also symbols of leadership and prestige.

The hei tiki, a human-form pendant, is one of the most well-known Māori adornments. This 18th- or 19th-century example is made from pounamu, or greenstone, from Westland in the South Island.

MĀORI WEAVING – NGĀ MAHI A HINETEIWAIWA

The first Polynesian settlers also imported their knowledge of weaving, along with aute, paper mulberry, a plant whose inner bark was used for making cloth in their tropical homeland. But growing aute was always difficult here, even in the warmest regions.

The settlers found a wide range of long-leaved plants, vines, reeds and barks for their fibre craft. But harakeke, New Zealand flax, was the new wonder plant. Common almost everywhere and highly versatile, it was put to a host of uses, from the everyday to the exceptional.

The long, tough leaves were stripped and woven into baskets, nets, coverings and sails. They were also scraped to reveal muka, the silken material inside. This high-grade fibre was used for fine weaving such as the soft fabrics of cloaks, as well as twine for cords and bindings. Harakeke was harvested in vast amounts by flax millers in the 19th and early 20th centuries. They produced a coarse grade of the fibre, which was exported to make ropes, mainly for ships.

Taonga (cultural treasures) made from plant materials are highly susceptible to decay. Sometimes mere fragments are all that remain to tell a story. Complete examples that are more than 100 years old are among the rarest of Te Papa's taonga. Conserving these materials is a highly specialised skill – and an essential one in the Museum.

The art of Māori weaving continues today. Knowledge about ancestral fibre craft, and the skills to create it, have been handed down through generations. The culture of preserving these skills, applying them and refining the technology is regarded as a taonga in itself.

This kahu huruhuru, or feather cloak, was woven in the 19th century by an unknown weaver from flax fibres and the feathers of eight different bird species: kererū, tūī, pūkeko, kākā, kākāriki, ruru, peacock and pheasant.

Te Papa Open Day visitors in Te Whare Pora o Hineteiwaiwa, Te Papa's Māori textile storeroom.

EUROPEAN EXPLORATION

Hundreds of years after the first people arrived, a new wave of explorers, this time from Europe, began to frequent the southern Pacific.

Abel Tasman's Dutch expedition was searching for the great southern continent that Europeans thought must exist. In 1642, they charted a strip of New Zealand's coastline and had a brief but bloody encounter with the local Māori.

In 1768, James Cook led a British expedition of scientific discovery for the Royal Society. He mapped New Zealand fully, identifying it as a group of islands rather than the seaboard of a huge continent.

Tupaia, a chief and skilled navigator, joined the expedition in Tahiti. As a Tahitian speaker, he could understand Māori, and his translation skills facilitated the first extended interaction between Europeans and Māori. Both groups gained a taste of new and peculiar worlds, and their encounters would change each other forever. Souvenirs from Cook's and other explorers' voyages generated huge excitement among collectors in Europe.

Once Europeans began settling in New Zealand, the transformation of the land accelerated. They brought with them steel tools and many new species of plants and animals. They also brought guns, which unleashed new levels of destruction in New Zealand.

'*Resolution* and *Adventure*' medals were distributed to indigenous people by James Cook and his men of the ships *Resolution* and *Adventure* during his second voyage of 1772–75.

Some of Europe's greatest navigators came to the Pacific in the 17th and 18th centuries, lured initially by rumours of a vast southern continent and then later to pursue scientific and imperial quests. The greatest was Captain James Cook, who made three significant voyages to the South Pacific between 1768 and 1779. He was killed on the last one, in Hawai'i. Te Papa holds this embroidered silk waistcoat, said to have belonged to him.

This cannon from Cook's ship the *Endeavour* is one of six recovered in 1969 from the Great Barrier Reef. Two hundred years earlier, the cannons were thrown overboard to lighten the *Endeavour*'s load to avoid it running aground on the perilous reef.

Made in France in 1760, this anchor from French explorer Jean de Surville's vessel *St Jean Baptiste* is one of the oldest European relics found in New Zealand. De Surville reached New Zealand in 1769 and anchored for two weeks in Doubtless Bay, where he lost this and two other anchors in a storm. This anchor was discovered by undersea explorer the late Kelly Tarlton, and donated to Te Papa in 1974. Made from wrought iron, it weighs nearly one and a half tonnes.

EUROPEAN SETTLERS

Many of the early European colonists were working men of a rough and ready type, attracted by accounts of plentiful raw materials needed back home: seals, which provided skin; whales, which provided oil; and tall timber for ship masts.

The newcomers had to negotiate access to these resources. They also needed food and water. The potato was now widely cultivated. Māori, with their communal resources, were quick to organise a surplus for trade. Guns, steel tools, tobacco and blankets were highly valued in exchange.

In order to facilitate trade, many of these early settlers learnt to speak the indigenous language, as did the highly active missionaries. In the early 19th century, this became known as Māori, which came from the expression tangata māori (ordinary people). Eventually, the word for ordinary or general came to identify the people themselves.

It was not just Europeans doing the exploring. Māori men became crew members on foreign ships, and others of high status began visiting the home countries of Europeans. Renowned Ngāpuhi leader Hongi Hika visited England in 1820. While there, he helped compile the first Māori dictionary, met King George IV, and traded various gifts for muskets with which to arm his tribe.

The rapid adoption and adaptation of materials, goods and ideas created upheaval during the 1820s and 1830s. The need for order became a key motivation for the Treaty of Waitangi, which formalised a relationship with the British government.

This New Zealand Company flag was made on the *Tory* during its voyage from England to New Zealand in 1839. It was raised at Petone at the northern end of Wellington harbour on 30 September by New Zealand Company agents intent on buying land from local Māori. Its design was based on a flag adopted by Māori chiefs at Waitangi in 1834 and known as the 'United Tribes of New Zealand' flag, which became a symbol of Māori independence.

The Treaty of Waitangi is the nation's founding document. In 1840, it was signed by Māori chiefs and representatives of the British Crown, sparking a period of intense settlement, mostly from Britain.

Many Māori viewed the Treaty as a sacred covenant that promised partnership with the British Crown and its governments. Over the decades, however, politicians and their settler electorate increasingly regarded the Treaty as irrelevant to the nation's progress.

Māori, struggling with the loss of their lands and other resources, were marginalised. Protesters cited the promises of the Treaty, but governments consistently ignored their claims, leading to a series of wars between Māori and the British in the 1860s. The conclusion of that war was bitter for many Māori: thousands of acres of land were taken by the Crown as a punishment for rebellion and what was left was gradually alienated by governments needing to satisfy settler hunger for farmland.

From the end of the 19th century, Māori began to promote their own social and cultural revival, but it was not until the 1970s that substantial political change came about. Today, there is an established process for investigating and dealing with Treaty of Waitangi claims by tribes, or iwi, through the Waitangi Tribunal. Over 50 have been settled, and many more are in negotiation. The process is often difficult but it is mostly regarded as positive and has given many iwi a new economic base. New Zealand commemorates the signing of its founding document on Waitangi Day (6 February), which was established as a public holiday in 1974.

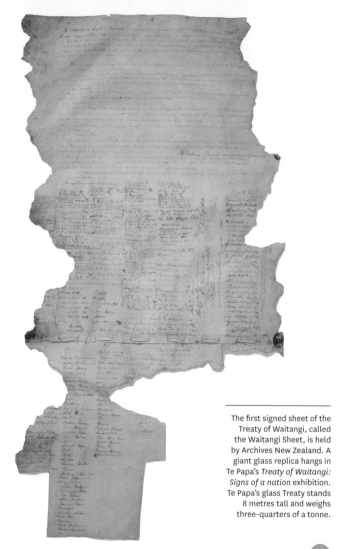

The first signed sheet of the Treaty of Waitangi, called the Waitangi Sheet, is held by Archives New Zealand. A giant glass replica hangs in Te Papa's *Treaty of Waitangi: Signs of a nation* exhibition. Te Papa's glass Treaty stands 8 metres tall and weighs three-quarters of a tonne.

NATION OF IMMIGRANTS

In the 1800s, most settlers to New Zealand came from the United Kingdom. These early immigrants faced months at sea, often in cramped discomfort. Most were English speakers. The majority of the people now known as Pākehā, European New Zealanders, trace their roots back to these or later immigrants from Britain.

British settlement in New Zealand continued throughout the 20th century. But added to the mix were significant numbers of settlers from other parts of the globe, such as Italy, Greece, India, the Pacific, Korea, the Philippines and Vietnam. More recently, large numbers of immigrants from mainland China have settled here.

The seeding of a new community might begin with an individual or a family. Soon, other relatives, friends, or neighbours are encouraged to follow their lead, and so discernible local groups form quickly.

Life in New Zealand today is composed of influences and contributions from all these groups and individuals. Te Papa has many objects in its collections – precious reminders of old homelands and grateful gifts to a new one – that help tell newcomers' stories.

► This black lacquer trunk belonging to Chinese settler Wong Tow still has its original carrying ropes and hessian wrapping. Wong Tow probably immigrated to New Zealand around 1900.

The European settlers brought their patterns of land use with them. Wetlands were drained, and enormous tracts of the remaining forest were felled or burned to create space and timber for settlements and farms.

For 19th-century Pākehā, big money could be made from the export of wool and, with the introduction of refrigerated transport, meat and dairy products. Timber was exported in bulk, and is still found in the elegant buildings of San Francisco and other major international cities. Until the late 1970s, New Zealand was Britain's 'farm in the south'.

There were also explosions in certain animal populations. Rabbits were introduced for hunting, but instead flourished and turned pasture to dust. Stoats and weasels were introduced to prey on rabbits but also feasted on native birds – to ruinous effect.

As a result of all these changes and intense economic activity, many ancient plants and animals disappeared, along with their habitats. Various species are still under threat today. It is almost impossible now to imagine the lost worlds of ancient New Zealand.

However, amid the clamour for prosperity, there were dissenting voices. Both Māori and Pākehā warned of the costs of exploitation. Many individuals – farmers, scientists and nature-loving citizens – spoke up about caring for the natural environment. By the 1970s, these voices had turned into mass protest movements, which have in turn led to a widespread awareness of the need for environmental balance.

► For decades New Zealand was Britain's 'farm in the south'. This 1930s wooden butter box shows the now-classic New Zealand fern-leaf symbol.

MASSEY

NEW ZEALAND PRODUCE

REG. Nº 16

NEW ZEALAND

56 LBS NET

PURE CREAMERY BUTTER

GLOBAL WARS

Sending national forces to fight in overseas wars has come at a considerable cost to New Zealand for over a century. Some 18,500 New Zealanders died during World War I, and another 50,000 were wounded — a total of seven percent of the country's population at the time.

Signing up to serve in that war was considered by many to be an adventure, a chance to fight for an Empire which still exerted strong emotional bonds in a nation not yet 80 years old. However the price these young soldiers paid was enormous, first at Gallipoli against the Ottoman Army, and then against the Germans on the Western Front.

New Zealand's involvement in the ill-fated Gallipoli campaign of 1915 is explored in the blockbuster exhibition *Gallipoli: The scale of our war*, developed by Te Papa working closely with Weta Workshop. It shows how important mates and memories of home were to men fighting in the grim industrialised warfare waged in Turkey, Sinai, France and Belgium. Afterwards, local war memorials – the focus for community services all around the country every 25 April, Anzac Day – helped New Zealanders make sense of war-time deaths.

Later, New Zealanders would distinguish themselves through their significant involvement in World War II, and then conflicts in South-East Asia from the 1950s to 1970s.

Since then, the New Zealand Defence Force has often been deployed in peacekeeping activities and military operations in the Pacific, Africa, Asia, Europe and the Middle East.

This World War I identity disc brooch belonged to 22-year-old Taranaki man Morris Brown. It was sent back to his family after he was killed in action at Gallipoli on 2 May 1915.

Te Papa's ground-breaking exhibition *Gallipoli: The scale of our war*, developed by Te Papa working closely with Weta Workshop, opened in April 2015. It tells the story of the Gallipoli campaign in World War I through the eyes and words of eight ordinary New Zealanders, each captured frozen in a moment of time on a monumental scale – 2.4 times human size.

It took Weta Workshop 24,000 hours to make the large, detailed sculptures in the *Gallipoli* exhibition.

BEING 'KIWI'

After the Treaty of Waitangi was signed, a new notion of New Zealand — and later 'Kiwi' — identity evolved.

Integral to the developing New Zealand identity was, and remains, a commitment to social justice. Kiwis live in a broadly egalitarian society and believe that everyone deserves a 'fair go'. In recent times, the same economic stresses that are felt throughout the Western world have frayed some of that egalitarianism but most New Zealanders are determined that it be preserved.

After all, it's a long legacy. In 1893, New Zealand became the first country in the world to give women full voting rights, and in the 1930s a Labour government pioneered a raft of social reforms, including the provision of free health care for all.

In recent decades, the pursuit of a fair go has seen Māori, women and gay people stand up for their rights. Widespread protests staged against the Vietnam War, apartheid sport and nuclear testing in the Pacific have reflected Kiwis' willingness to oppose injustice or back a principle. In 1985, New Zealanders made a bold assertion of independence: visits by nuclear ships were banned, and New Zealand was declared 'nuclear free'. This caused diplomatic ructions with the US, but the policy was popular locally. New Zealand remains nuclear free.

Rights for homosexual New Zealanders were a focus of campaigning from the mid 1980s, and gay marriage became legal in 2013.

► This badge encapsulates the anti-nuclear sentiment that became a uniting and defining principle for Kiwis through the 1970s, 1980s and beyond. It was created in 1981 by Lawrence Ross, who coordinated the successful campaign to achieve the Nuclear Free Zone policy in 1987. Te Papa has an extensive collection of protest objects from the past 160 years.

NUCLEAR WEAPON FREE ZONE
NEW ZEALAND

Isolated from the rest of the world geographically, the first settlers – Māori and European – developed unique characteristics, just as the local flora and fauna did.

To survive, those pioneering folk had to be resilient and determined. They had to adapt, improvise and innovate. Te Papa houses many items that attest to this inventiveness – a quality much in evidence in today's population. Popular legend has it that Kiwis can fix just about anything with the clever application of some number 8 fencing wire.

Farming has always been vital to New Zealand – both culturally and economically – and New Zealanders have created a number of innovative rural solutions. Portable electric fencing is one example of an invention that has influenced farming methods worldwide.

Innovation sometimes manifests itself in groups of people, such as Māori families who pass on customary knowledge through generations. Equally, some locations have become creative hothouses; Wellington, where Weta Workshop is based, is world-renowned for film-industry excellence.

A handful of individual innovators have achieved global recognition. They include flying-machine inventor Richard Pearse; Burt Munro, who set several land-speed records on his modified Indian motorcycle; and Bill Hamilton, whose jet boats navigated shallow and fast-flowing rivers. In 1960, a Hamilton Jet boat became the first craft to travel up the Colorado River through the Grand Canyon.

► John Britten's revolutionary V1000 racing motorcycle is regarded as a contemporary classic of motorcycle design. Driven to build the fastest four-stroke motorcycle in the world, Britten designed an aerodynamic, light-weight engineering marvel. Built in 1992, Te Papa's Britten bike is the second of only 10 in the world.

A popular Kiwi stereotype is a bloke who works on a farm, wears a black T-shirt and gumboots, and lives and breathes rugby. This caricature still holds some currency, but the Kiwi has evolved into a more sophisticated and diverse species. Today's New Zealander is just as likely to be innovative with a modem cable as with number 8 wire. And while most Kiwis love sporting pursuits and the great outdoors, many more live in urban than rural areas.

Many New Zealanders have travelled extensively and lived in other countries. Wherever they are, New Zealanders retain a strong identity, reflected in popular icons such as the silver fern. Their English has its own sound and its own content, with some strong influence from te reo Māori (Māori language). Home or abroad they feel a strong affinity with the land.

They also feel immense pride when fellow citizens achieve on the world stage – especially given the country's small population: Nobel laureate Sir Ernest Rutherford, writer Katherine Mansfield, aviator Jean Batten, yachtsman Sir Peter Blake, mountaineer Sir Edmund Hillary, opera diva Dame Kiri Te Kanawa, pop singer Lorde, actors Sam Neill and Jermaine Clement, fashion designers Karen Walker and WORLD, novelist Eleanor Catton, director Sir Peter Jackson, and of course a host of talented, world-beating All Blacks, are but a few.

► Te Papa holds the iconic 'Pearl' dress by internationally renowned New Zealand fashion designer Karen Walker. It was presented at Mercedes Australian Fashion Week in 2000.

Te Papa's
largest
collection item is the
24-metre yacht
NZL32 Black Magic,
winner
of the 1995
America's Cup
in San Diego.*

*Currently on long-term display at the New Zealand
Maritime Museum in Auckland.

The smallest
collection item
is a microscopic
water bear
(tardigrade)
specimen, only
0.162 millimetres long.

PACIFIC INFLUENCE

Geographically, New Zealand is a Pacific country, whose human history is shared with the peoples of that ocean.

In the late 19th and early 20th centuries, government leaders dreamed of creating an empire in the Pacific – and so brought Samoa, the Cook Islands and Niue under New Zealand rule.

Those relationships opened doors to the establishment of Pacific Island communities here. From the 1950s, immigration swelled in response to acute labour shortages in New Zealand.

Members of these communities have become notable achievers in all spheres of New Zealand life. Rugby legends Jerome Kaino, Tana Umaga and the late Jonah Lomu; politician Luamanuvao Winnie Laban; Commonwealth Writers' Prize winner Albert Wendt; poet Selina Tusitala Marsh; shot putter Valerie Adams; and hip-hop artist King Kapisi are just a few.

Pacific influences and unique expressions of cultural fusion abound in New Zealand, for example, in fashion, art, the 'Pacific sound' in music and the practice of tattoo. Many New Zealanders now see themselves as Pacific people.

► Te Papa's Pacific Cultures Collection represents history from first human settlement through to the present day. This 18th-century 'aumakua hulu manu is considered to represent the Hawaiian war god, Kūkā'ilimoku. It is made from feathers attached to a net-lined wickerwork frame, with dog teeth and pearl shell eyes.

This vaka (outrigger canoe) from Manihiki in the northern Cook Islands is one of only three such vaka that survive in museums worldwide. Made from wood lashed together with sennit (coconut husk fibre) and decorated with inlaid pieces of pearl shell, it is called *Tauhunu* after the main village on Manihiki. It was bought for the Dominion Museum, Te Papa's predecessor, in 1907.

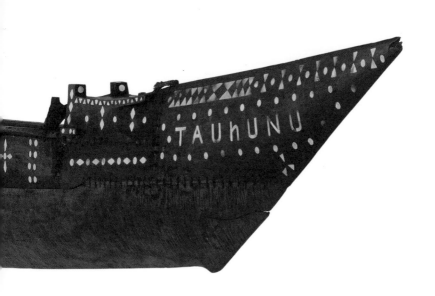

Michel Tuffery's (1966–) 1994 sculpture *Pisupo lua afe (Corned beef 2000)* comments on the influences of trade on Pacific people's lives. Imported corned beef, known as pisupo, has replaced local foods to become a staple of the Pacific diet, contributing to a decline in fishing and cultivation, and to poor health.

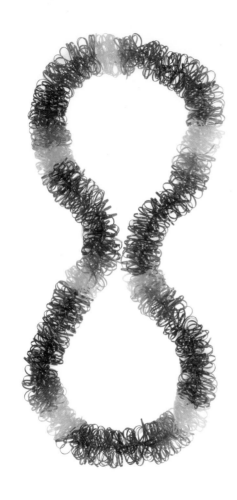

Niki Hastings-McFall's (1959–) *Weedeater lei*, created in 2000, is a playful example of a modern lei (neck adornment). Originally, lei symbolised status and were made from feathers, flowers, seeds, shells, leaves and, sometimes, precious whale's teeth. Today, Pacific communities in New Zealand continue to make lei from the materials available to them, including brightly coloured plastics or wrapped sweets.

Te Papa's most travelled exhibition is *Whales / Tohorā*, which opened in 2007 and is still touring overseas today.

The one-tonne piece of **greenstone** in the marae is called **Tongarewa** and represents the **life force** of Te Papa.

A MEETING OF ART TRADITIONS

New Zealanders are the inheritors of two great art traditions. One links back to the ancestral world of Polynesia. The other originates in Europe, with roots in the classical world of Greece and Rome.

Māori artists were quick to adapt Western tools, materials and ideas. By the 1850s, striking innovations in painting, weaving and sculpture had emerged. These are seen in the buildings and carved or woven taonga (cultural treasures) that are the special expression of Māori identity – and also the marrying of indigenous culture with imported technology.

Most Pākehā artists continued within the main conventions of their tradition, as many immigrants do. They did, however, include Māori subjects and the New Zealand landscape in their works. Their content, if not their style, was identifiably local. There was a flourishing market for such depictions, both here and in Britain.

From the 1860s, photography became widespread. The camera, a revolutionary new device, could capture instantly a spectacular and rapidly changing land – as well as its human face. Photographic portraits quickly became important to Māori as memorials of the dead. Such photos often feature in funeral ceremonies or tangi and are hung on meeting house walls.

► *Maori girl*, painted in about 1874, was one of Gottfried Lindauer's (1839–1926) many commissioned portraits.

Hot Water Cups White Terrace
C. Spencer Photo Nº 16

Te Papa holds many important early photographs, including Charles Spencer's (1854–1933) *Hot Water Cups, White Terrace*, photographed in the 1880s, before this top tourist destination near Rotorua was destroyed by the eruption of nearby Mount Tarawera in 1886.

NEW DIRECTIONS IN ART

By the end of the 19th century, the old certainties of Western art traditions were eroding under the influence of new movements. In the early 20th century, many talented, Western-trained artists left New Zealand to engage with the modern art movements in Europe.

Some returned to New Zealand, but many did not. They felt the local artistic environment was too conservative and unsupportive. However, they continued to exhibit here, helping to inform those at home about new approaches.

At the same time, politician and cultural leader Sir Āpirana Ngata was concerned that the knowledge of traditional arts was declining among Māori. From the 1920s, he championed a new generation of Māori artists, who focused their expression on the wharenui, the meeting house.

In the mid-1930s, many Pākehā artists felt that New Zealand art had to start anew. Their work was rooted in a land far away from Europe. They acknowledged their New Zealand birth and heritage, but they also looked for new, revitalising ideas from abroad. Abstracting the landscape was one response. Another was interpreting Māori art from the perspective of European modernism.

Māori artists also looked beyond the traditional. From the 1950s, a new generation began expressing their cultural knowledge and experience through Western art forms.

In more recent times, globalisation has created worldwide opportunities for artists to exhibit their work. It has also stimulated a powerful interest in authentic expressions of indigenous identity, as evidenced by the international market for the work of contemporary Māori artists.

Paratene Matchitt (1933–, Ngāti Porou, Te Whānau ā Apanui, Te Whakatōhea) is known for combining traditional Māori art forms with those of modernist art. His 1962 painting *Whiti te ra* is a cubist interpretation of Māori motifs. Its title references the closing phrase of the famous 'Ka mate' haka, composed by warrior chief Te Rauparaha, suggesting a triumphant figure at the moment of cheating death.

Influential jeweller Warwick Freeman (1953–) came to prominence in the late 1980s as part of the Bone Stone Shell jewellery movement, which moved away from European influences and drew on local and Pacific cultures and materials. This pearl shell brooch, *Large star*, was made in 1990.

At the same time as New Zealand jewellers were experimenting with new materials and methods, New Zealand glass artists began to explore the potential of glass. Ann Robinson (1944–), whose 2001 *Ice Bowl* is shown here, is one of New Zealand's most innovative and highly regarded glass artists.

Northland panels by Colin McCahon (1919–1987), one of New Zealand's most significant painters, depicts eight scenes from rural Northland. Painted in 1958, its large scale and loose, expressive style were influenced by McCahon's tour of the United States, where he saw large abstract paintings by contemporary artists, including Jackson Pollock, Mark Rothko and Willem de Kooning.

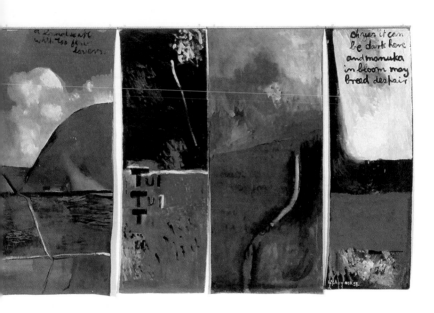

a landscape
with too few
lovers.

Tui
Tui
T

chries it can
be dark here
and manuka
in bloom may
breed despair

Michael Parekowhai (1968–, Ngā Ariki and Ngāti Whakarongo) created *He Korero Purakau mo Te Awanui o Te Motu: Story of a New Zealand river* as the central work of his 2011 Venice Biennale installation. Made from a Steinway concert piano, it took more than 10 years to create, and references the seminal New Zealand novel by Jane Mander.

He Poroporoakī

A Word of Farewell

We hope you've enjoyed your journey through Te Papa. Please keep in touch.

Visit our website, catch up on Facebook, Twitter and Instagram, and see our collections online.

Friends of Te Papa offers you unique opportunities and experiences at the Museum, and the Te Papa Foundation enables you to support our work.

Check out the excellent range of products in our online store. Every purchase helps our exhibitions, scholarship and programmes.

We wish you well.

Haere rā. Goodbye.

www.tepapa.govt.nz

IMAGE CREDITS

All photography by Te Papa photographers Michael Hall, Norm Heke, Mike O'Neill, Jean-Claude Stahl, Kate Whitley and Jan Nauta unless otherwise credited. All scanning and digital imaging by Jeremy Glyde.

Registration numbers are provided for collection items illustrated in this guide. Further information on these objects can be found at http://collections.tepapa.govt.nz.

Page 9 PH001887; **29** AI.000632; **30** SP063797/A; **31** P009454/A; **35** M.077205/M.136281-2/M.136293; **36** OR.010143; **37 from top** LM001329, OR.025020; **38** S.023700; **39** LM000760; **41 from top** P.035420, photographed by Andrew Stewart, Te Papa; P.032901, photographed by Andrew Stewart, Te Papa; P.050498, photographed by Carl Struthers, Te Papa; P.049400, photographed by Carl Struthers, Te Papa; **42–3** M.190318; **44** GH004839; **45 left** FE003200; **from top** TMP004028, TMP002175; both on loan from the National Paleontological Collections, GNS Science, Lower Hutt; **49** ME015920; **50–1** ME012263; **53** ME001771; **55** ME004211; **56** ME010922; **57** ME023984; **59** ME011987; **63** GH024769; **64** PC001529; **65 from top** DM000477, NS000047/2; **67** GH002925; **69** photograph courtesy of Archives New Zealand; **71** GH004850/1; **73** GH010066; **75** GH024229; **81** GH011812; **83** T000649; **85** GH009488; **89** FE000325; **90–1** FE010421; **92** FE010516; **93** FE011580; **97** 1936-0036-1; **98–9** O.000766/1; **101** 2003-0019-1; **102** 2002-0016-2; **103** 2002-0030-1; **104–5** 1978-0009-1, courtesy of the Colin McCahon Research and Publication Trust; **106–7** 2011-0046-1.

GLOSSARY OF TE REO MĀORI TERMS

kaihautū	leader in partnership with the chief executive of Te Papa
karanga	ceremonial call of welcome to visitors onto a marae
mana	prestige, authority, influence, spiritual power
marae	courtyard in front of a wharenui; in modern times all the buildings and the land are referred to as the 'marae'
Matariki	Māori New Year, Pleiades or Seven Sisters star cluster
mātauranga	knowledge
pā	fortified village, or in modern times a Māori community
pounamu	greenstone
pōwhiri	welcome ceremony on a marae
taonga	treasure, object
waharoa	traditional entranceway to a fortified village, to a marae, or in modern times a city
wharenui	meeting house

First published in 2017 by Te Papa Press
PO Box 467, Wellington, New Zealand
www.tepapapress.co.nz

Based on a text by Michael Keith

TE PAPA

PRESS

TE PAPA® is the trademark of the Museum
of New Zealand Te Papa Tongarewa
Te Papa Press is an imprint of the Museum
of New Zealand Te Papa Tongarewa

A catalogue record is available from the National
Library of New Zealand

ISBN 978-0-9941362-2-0

Design by Kate Barraclough
Printed in China by 1010 Printing International Limited

Front cover image: The Museum from Cable Street, Wellington.